T0199168

Harriet's
STORY

PEG CRAIG

WestBow Press books may be ordered through booksellers or by contacting:

WestBow Press
A Division of Thomas Nelson & Zondervan
1663 Liberty Drive
Bloomington, IN 47403
www.westbowpress.com
1 (866) 928-1240

ISBN: 978-1-9736-5989-1 (sc)
ISBN: 978-1-9736-5990-7 (e)

Library of Congress Control Number: 2019904229

Print information available on the last page.

WestBow Press rev. date: 06/13/2019

WestBow
PRESS®
A DIVISION OF THOMAS NELSON
& ZONDERVAN

HARRIET'S STORY

PEG CRAIG

CHAPTER 1

THE STORY BEGINS

Eight year old Harriet was ready to leave. The carriage would be coming soon. Her father and stepmother had packed all they could take with them in a small trunk. War had come to Wilmington, North Carolina where her father, the Rev. Jonathan Allan Wainwright, was the Rector of St. John's Episcopal Church and they had to leave immediately to return to Connecticut. Harriet was leaving behind all her things, except her favorite doll. Her father said she could bring it if she carried it – there was no room in the trunk.

So began a family story that now spans seven generations. Pieces of it have been saved by various family members along with some remarkable photographs. But until now there has been no narrative to link these memories together. This is my gift to Harriet's descendants as I have been privileged to have been given the pieces and have had the time and inclination to organize these memories.

I first heard about Harriet from my mother Katharine Cook Orwig. Harriet was her grandmother and lived with her family during her last years of life. My mother told me the story of her grandmother and her doll and about her birth in what was then the western frontier, now in the state of Iowa. Later, when I was still a small girl, my mother took me to visit Harriet's sister Katharine Wainwright Mackey in Palmyra, Missouri. She was born in 1864 and was my mother's great aunt. My mother always called her "Aunt Katharine" so I will too. Aunt Katharine Mackey kept records of family history and made scrapbooks for her great-nieces and nephews. I have some of these scrapbooks which have provided the primary sources to tell this remarkable story. Therefore this family history does not consist of legends passed down through many tellers but in her writings Aunt Katharine gives us a firsthand account of Harriet's life. I am letting her tell her stories to the grandchildren of my cousins in the Cook family and my second cousins in the Evans family all of whom are alive because Harriet escaped from the South, married and raised two children, John Wainwright Evans and Gertrude Evans Cook, who are the grandparents of these cousins. Some of Dick Jones' grandchildren will be reading this story. Dick sat on her lap for a picture when she was an old lady. So it really wasn't so long ago.

This picture was taken around 1936. Richard H. Jones is sitting on the lap of his great-grandmother, Harriet Wainwright Evans

In order to understand the story of Harriet's trip from Wilmington and the special story of her doll, we need to go back in time and begin with the story of how Harriet happened to be born in Iowa before the Civil War. Harriet's father, Jonathan Allen Wainwright, was born in Plattsburg, New York on the shore of Lake Champlain on October 24, 1821. I am writing this in 2019 so that was almost 200 years ago. His father was Alfred Wainwright. His mother was Clarissa Foote. In 1907, a distant cousin wrote a family history of the descendants of Nathaniel Foote.[1] In this history we learn that Clarissa was born February 17, 1795. Her father, Freeman, belonged to the Vermont Volunteers during the Revolutionary War. Aunt Katharine says that he served with the Green Mountain Boys under Ethan Allen which was why Jonathan's middle name was Allen.

Before the Revolutionary War the land which is now Vermont was claimed by both the colonies of New York and New Hampshire. The Green Mountain Boys militia was set up to resist takeovers from New York. One of the leaders was Ethan Allen. Early in the Revolutionary War they seized Fort Ticonderoga from the British in a surprise raid. Aunt Katharine says that Freeman Foote participated in that event. Later Ethan Allen was captured by the British and held for much of the war. In 1777 Vermont declared itself as an independent republic until it finally entered the United States as the 14th state in 1791.

Clarissa had a cousin named Roxanna who married into the Beecher family. Roxanna's son, Henry Ward Beecher, was a famous preacher. Her daughter, Harriet Beecher, married Calvin Stowe and wrote *Uncle Tom's Cabin*. This is the closest we've come to being related to anyone famous.

Harriet Beecher Stowe's book, though a fictional account, "had a profound effect on attitudes toward African Americans and slavery."[2] It is said that when Abraham Lincoln met her he said, "So you are the little lady that started this great war" because her book had made the Northerners ready to fight to end slavery.[3]

Clarissa Foote married Alfred Wainwright in 1814. She had three daughters and then in 1821 Jonathan was born. But six months later, on April 22, 1822, Clarissa died. At her funeral the preacher said, "Undoubtedly, the inclination to literature was brought to the family by Clarissa Foote. As far as my experience goes, this is a marked characteristic."[4]

In 1823 Alfred Wainwright married Clarissa's sister, Delia. Soon afterward Alfred moved his family to Montpelier, Vermont. There he established an iron foundry in 1832 to produce iron goods, particularly those used for agriculture.[5]

Alfred's son, Jonathan Wainwright, always believed that he was called to the ministry, but his father wanted him to be a doctor. In that time, parents had a great deal of control over the choices of their children, so despite his desires, Jonathan graduated from the University of Vermont in 1846 and enrolled at Castleton Medical College. He received his medical degree three years later. While he was still in Castleton he met Harriet Hayden of Torringford, Connecticut.

Cicero Hayden, Harriet's father, owned a brick-making company in Torrington, Connecticut. He and his wife Sophia Squires Hayden had eight children and Harriet was the third of the four sisters. Her oldest sister, Sophia, was the principal of Castleton Seminary in Vermont, one of the early schools for women in New England. It was related to Castleton Medical College and when she was old enough, Harriet enrolled there.

Harriet Hayden Wainwright, mother of Harriet Wainwright. Date unknown.

Aunt Katharine wrote that her grandfather, Jonathan Wainwright, studied cases of ship's fever (now called typhus) while he was in medical school and contracted the disease, which caused him to lose his hair, resulting in an amusing account of his courtship. Aunt Katharine writes, "He was incapacitated for many months and lost all his hair. He wore a very attractive wig and during this period met Harriet Hayden. The couple became engaged and later he went to the Hayden home at Torringford. Jonathan and Harriette were sitting on the west stone step when Caroline, youngest daughter of the family, peeked out of the window above and at once discovered the wig. Later she twitted her sister who vehemently denied the insinuation. Caroline told her brother Henry to make some excuse to go to the guest's room after he retired. He did. The wig hung on a chair."

Jonathan married Harriet Hayden sometime in the spring of 1850. They moved to Davenport, Iowa, which was the frontier in those pre-Civil War days. He entered into a partnership with Dr. E.S. Barrows, a physician and surgeon. The Barrows house is now a museum in Davenport.

After they settled in Davenport there was a cholera epidemic. Aunt Katharine writes that Jonathan was "often so exhausted he lay down anywhere to catch a moment's sleep. He said 'more people died from fear than cholera', coffins could not be made fast enough to supply the demand." Harriet was expecting her first child and on September 22, 1853 their baby daughter was born and named Harriet, after her mother. Tragedy struck and two days later the new mother died. Baby Harriet's Aunt Sophia Hayden, who had come to help her sister with the new baby, was also very ill with the fever yet survived to take care of the tiny, premature baby who weighed only three pounds.

Aunt Katharine tells the story of Harriet Wainwright's first train trip. "Some weeks later, on a small pillow, tiny baby Harriette who hardly filled a quart cup, started by railroad coach and slow moving train, back to her mother's New England home. There were no Pullman coaches, dining cars or refrigerators in those days. The conductor obligingly stopped the train and milked a cow for her benefit."

The names are confusing because the baby's name was the same as her mother's and because sometimes Aunt Katharine calls her "Harriette" and sometimes "Hattie". From now on, all references to Harriet Wainwright will be to our great-grandmother, not to her mother.

CHAPTER 2

HARRIET'S FAMILY

This is a picture of the house at the end of Hayden Hill Road. 1941.

Aunt Katharine had several pictures of the Hayden home in Connecticut taken in different years in her scrapbooks. About thirty years ago I traveled to Torringford to see if I could find it. I found a filling station at the crossroads marked on the map as Torringford and showed a picture to the attendant. He did not recognize it, but sent me to see the owner of a neighboring business saying that she knew something about local history. She studied the picture and then said she thought she knew where it was. She told us to turn north and go to where the road was crossed by "Hayden Hill Road." We did and found it there. It is actually two houses built next to each other, one of wood and one of brick.

The wooden house was built by Harriet Wainwright's great-grandfather Augustin Hayden. He was born in eastern Connecticut in 1740 and at 18 he enlisted in "His Majesty's service" to fight the French and their Native American allies. He fought to take Fort Ticonderoga on Lake Champlain.

This was during what was known as the French and Indian War when the French allied themselves with the Native Americans to take England's lands in America. It was part of a larger conflict between the two European countries. The British also had allies among the natives. It started as a conflict over the land that is now Pittsburgh, Pennsylvania and the fighting began when Virginia militiamen under the command of 22 year old George Washington ambushed a French patrol in 1754. Fort Ticonderoga was built by the French at the beginning of the war and called Fort Carillon. After the British captured it in 1759, with the assistance of Augustin Hayden, it was renamed Fort Ticonderoga.[6] It remained in British control until the Green Mountain Boys seized it in 1775 with the help of Freeman Foote.

Augustin Hayden kept a diary of his time as a soldier[7]. In the summer of 1758 he wrote with imaginative spelling, "We got up to the Narrows and landed that day. Before night we took about one 150 Prisonors and kild some. We lost sum but not menny Lord How [Brigadier General Lord Howe, effective commander of the expedition] was kild in the taking of those Prisonors." The next day they attacked Fort Carillon but did not succeed. They continued to fight with French units and on August 8 he recorded the capture of Israel Putnam. In late fall his enlistment was up and he returned to Windsor, Connecticut for the winter.

Lord George Howe had learned from the famous ranger Major Robert Rogers that the usual British uniforms and tactics were a disadvantage in frontier fighting. The uniforms were cut short and all lace was removed. Their hair was cut short. His army trained in fighting in the woods until they were as skilled as the rangers.[8] His British troops were accompanied by Augustin's unit of Connecticut Militia with Israel Putnam as a scout and guide. Israel Putnam would be the hero of the Battle of Bunker Hill during the Revolutionary War.[9]

The following spring Augustin reenlisted and set out again. That summer the French left the forts in the Lake Champlain area and the British, along with Augustin, moved in to them.

Aunt Katharine writes, "In passing through the site of Torringford on two campaigns, [Augustin] was greatly impressed with the beauty of a certain hill and determined then, when out of service he would build a home on its crest. This he did. He married Cynthea Filer of Windsor and in the frame part of the home at Torringford, became the father of fifteen children." There is no record of further journals or military service. Aunt Katharine hints that he might have been a Tory (British sympathizer). She also says that his uniform is in the museum at Hartford, but they haven't any record of it.

The brick house, "kitty corner" to the wooden house, was built by Augustin's youngest son, Cicero, Harriet's grandfather. The Hayden genealogy says, "His literary taste, averse to farm life, led him in 1807 to commence the study of law. Failing health soon compelled him to leave the office, and returning to the homestead passed his life in farming and the manufacture of brick. No matter how hurried the daily duties, the Bible was not only read but expounded every morning after breakfast. He was prosperous in business, of strict integrity, untiring energy, and perseverance. He was a man of decided opinions, which he vigorously defended. He was an early abolitionist, a strong temperance advocate, and in later years much given to the consideration of moral and religious subjects. He never sought office, though many times filling places of trust. When informed of his election to represent the town in the Legislature, he was unaware that he had been a candidate. A warm-hearted, genial man, his house was the abode of true hospitality, where rich and poor were alike welcome."[10]

Cicero and Sophia Squires Hayden, grandparents of Harriet Wainwright.

Aunt Katharine writes of her grandmother, Sophia Squires Hayden, "Grandma was the cheery, self-sacrificing mother, always bustling about." She also writes of their home. "The big room with its fireplace and bake oven was of course the gathering place. If the fire went out, a covered pan with a handle was sent to a neighbor for live coals. There were fireplaces in every room, but for the children a warming pan pushed between the sheets was the only heat. In the winter, snow banked up to the second story window, became packed and then the sleds came out, starting out of a window and then on down the long hill. The boys and hired men shoveled a tunnel to the barn to feed and water the stock." Sophia's obituary says, "Who can tell the joys and sorrows, the cares and pleasures she experienced in conducting her large household? How changed is that home since the days of yore! Then it was filled with bustle and business; its rooms were alive with youth and frolic; it was ever the abode of hospitality, and a favorite resort of young people, and none enjoyed their merry makings more heartily than did 'Uncle Cicero' and his genial and sprightly wife."[11]

But by the time tiny baby Harriet Wainwright arrived from Iowa, most of the children were grown up and gone from the home. Her youngest aunt, Caroline, was likely there and her oldest aunt, Amelia, never married and stayed at the family home.

Jonathan Wainwright, Harriet's father, stayed behind in Iowa. Even though both the Wainwrights and the Haydens were members of the Congregational Church, Dr. Wainwright was confirmed on June 1, 1854 at Davenport by the Rt. Rev. Jackson Kemper, first Episcopal Missionary Bishop on the frontier. Jonathan's father had died in 1852 so he returned to his first desire – to become a minister. He returned east and enrolled in the General Theological Seminary in New York City. During his studies he took a hiatus and became a tutor near

Vicksburg, Mississippi for two years, returning to the seminary to continue his studies. Jonathan was ordained a deacon at the famous Trinity Episcopal Church on Wall Street in New York City on June 27, 1858. My sister, Anne, has his ordination certificate. During his studies he stayed in touch with the Hayden family who were raising baby Harriet, and in 1858 married Caroline Hayden, one of Harriet Wainwright's aunts. This was the same sister that had discovered that he wore a wig. She was 27 by then, old to be still unmarried and she had already had an adventurous life.

Caroline's daughter, Katharine Mackey, writes, "Carrie Hayden [Caroline], was called by her father, the butterfly of the family – very proud, very ambitious, with abounding vitality. A description of her given me by one who had known her from childhood was, 'very beautiful, with white skin, rosy cheeks, dark brown eyes and hair, with very white teeth.' She went to Hartford for the 'polishing off' education, which meant French, music, painting, geography of the heavens, and mythology, all of them a very definite part of her life, as also was poetry."

Continuing her account of her mother's life, Aunt Katharine writes, "Carrie taught in the south several years. She was in Georgia when Charles Sumner, antislavery Senator from Massachusetts, made his speech on the 'Crime against Kansas' and Preston Brooks of South Carolina struck him senseless with a cane as he sat alone at his desk in the Senate chamber. She burst out at the table when all were at dinner, 'It was cowardly to come up and strike him from behind.' This was of course a bombshell. The next day she received a note, giving her a dismissal from her position. She said she was perfectly willing to go but she would expect her salary. This was refused. She went to no less a person than Alexander Stephens, Georgia Congressman and later Vice-President of the Confederacy. He showed his chivalry to this attractive young Yankee by winning her case. She got her salary."

CHAPTER 3

THE ESCAPE

Jonathan Wainwright's first church – then St. Philip's Episcopal, now Chapel of the Holy Cross.

You may be wondering how the Wainwright family, with roots firmly in the North, got to North Carolina in the mid-1800's. Our story continues here. After Jonathan was ordained as an Episcopal deacon, he accepted a position at St. Philip's Episcopal church at Fort Johnson located in what is now Southport, North Carolina where the Fear River empties into the Atlantic Ocean south of Wilmington. The Church had been built in 1843 to serve the troops at Fort Johnson in what was then known as Smithville. The History of St. Philip's says that Smithville was the first resort town in North Carolina and attracted summer residents because of its delightful climate. The original building is still there and is known as the Chapel of the Cross which was the name given to it when it was first built before the parish of St. Philip's was formed. The congregation has built a larger sanctuary across the street. Both structures are still used for worship.

Wilmington was the main port city, located about thirty miles up the Fear River. It was a growing, prosperous city with a new opera house. The congregation of St. James Episcopal church had outgrown its building and members determined that a second congregation should be formed and named after St. John, brother to St. James. The church history says, "The most urgent order of business was securing a rector. Bishop Atkinson suggested The Rev. J. A. Wainwright, M.D., a 39-year old deacon in Smithville [now Southport]. It was his first position since graduating from seminary in 1858, having given up the practice of medicine. Dr. Wainwright agreed to take the post for one year for a salary of $1,000 with the understanding that the contract would end after one year unless both parties wanted to continue it. He was ordained to the priesthood at St. John's May 17, 1860."[12]

Bell cast in 1860 – from St. John's Episcopal Church – Wilmington, North Carolina

The congregation still exists but the original church, built on third and Red Cross Streets in downtown Wilmington, is no longer standing. The congregation of St. John's moved in 1955 to a new church at 1219 Forest Hills Dr. in a newer area of town. But they brought the bell from the original building. This bell had been dedicated during the short tenure that Wainwright was Rector. The members built a new bell tower and still use the bell to call the faithful to worship. In 2016 my sister, Anne Weatherholt (also an Episcopal priest), my husband Bill and I visited St. John's and donated a Sanctus Bell in memory of our great-great-grandfather, whose picture is on the wall with other former Rectors. The Sanctus Bell is a gift from his descendants.

Harriet was almost seven years old when they moved to Wilmington. At some point she was given a lovely doll to keep her company. There was no plastic in those days so dolls for younger children were made of wood or cloth. Harriet's doll had a fabric or leather body but the head and possibly the hands and feet were made of china and painted with features. Girls needed to be careful when playing with these dolls because the china could be chipped or even broken if they were dropped or hit against something. The heads of china dolls were hollow and pierced with small holes at the neck where they were sewn on to the body of the doll.

Because she was so young, Harriet was probably unaware of the political turmoil which was to lead to the Civil War. Even though originally slaves had been owned in all parts of the colonies, and at least one of our ancestors owned a slave,[13] by 1860 slavery had been abolished in the states north of the Mason-Dixon Line dividing Maryland from Pennsylvania. Abolitionists like Jonathan's cousin, Harriet Beecher Stowe, had brought the evils of slavery to the attention of northerners and they resisted laws which compelled them to assist slave catchers looking for runaways. The nation was expanding to the west and people in the north did not want slavery to spread to new settlements, while the

Southerners wanted to bring their slaves in to the adjacent farming areas. At that time each state still thought of itself as an independent state united with other states when it benefitted them all, rather like the European Union is now. Abraham Lincoln was not even on the ballot in ten southern states but he won the presidency in 1860. Before he was inaugurated in March 1861 seven southern states had decided they would be better off without the north and seceded to form the Confederate States of America, known as the "Confederacy". The remaining states in the "Union" did not accept the declarations of secession and the current President, James Buchanan, refused to give up the forts in the area claimed by the Confederacy. Abraham Lincoln was inaugurated in March 1861. In April, Confederate troops fired on Fort Sumter in the harbor at Charleston, South Carolina and the fort surrendered a day later, starting the Civil War. In May, a year after the Wainwright family moved to Wilmington, North Carolina seceded and joined the Confederacy.

Harriet Wainwright as a girl – age unknown.

The church history tells what happened in Wilmington. "War fever infected every aspect of Wilmington life. Civil authorities asked all the ministers to include a prayer for the success of the Confederacy. Without discussing it with the vestry, Dr. Wainwright, a native of Plattsburg, N.Y., refused. Members of the vestry learned of their rector's misplaced patriotism second hand and were incensed. To make matters worse, the vestry had voted only weeks before to retain Dr. Wainwright permanently and he had accepted. Now this! Under cover of night in a closed carriage, members of the parish took Dr. and Mrs. Wainwright and their daughter to the train station to travel north."[14]

A current church member at St. John's supplied this information and reflected on the account. "I would like to give my opinion here as a 'born and raised' Southerner. It took a great deal of strength to stand up for what he believed in the middle of the times. I admire him very much and am so sorry it cost his family and him so much." She adds, "One things stands out to me. If there were 'members of the parish' who helped them escape, there were some people in the church who loved them enough to risk their lives to help them escape."[15]

This is why we found Harriet and her doll waiting for the carriage to come to take them to the train station when this story began. Aunt Katharine writes: "The fatal shot has been fired on Ft. Sumter. The Mason and Dixon Line has become a reality, bristling with musket and cannon. The world around the trip is ablaze. Locking the door on all their possessions – which they will never see again – they are fleeing with one canvas covered leather trunk, one doll and their wearing apparel, to the nearest exit thru the lines, Kentucky."

I've puzzled over this account for a number of years. The shortest route to New England would be towards the northeast. Traveling to Kentucky would mean going west to the Cumberland Gap, and tracing the Wilderness Road north to Cincinnati. From there they would have had to head northeast to Connecticut. It would have been a geographically difficult journey because the steep ridges of the Appalachians run from southwest to northeast with few places for railroad tracks to pass through. The mountains were sparsely settled then, with little to justify the expense of putting railroads through rough territory. Most railroad maps from that time show the lines running along the valleys. I have not found any record of a rail line across the mountains.

But if there was a route to the west it would have made sense to take it. Going directly north from Wilmington would have meant traveling through Richmond, Virginia the, capital of the Confederacy, not a safe place for fleeing refugees. The railroads were being used for transporting troops and supplies and were targets for both sides. Many of the battles during the war were centered on stations and rail lines. Jonathan was only forty years old at that time and would have attracted attention for not being in the military of either the North or the South. Most of their westbound trip would have been through North Carolina with only a short stretch through Tennessee before passing into the state of Kentucky which was not taking sides. Thus the long way around would have been safer.

In another account of the story, Aunt Katharine writes about her father, "The outbreak of the war between the states necessarily altered his plans. He thought at first that he could weather the storm and did not leave Wilmington until its full fury was upon him. The lines were closed and with one trunk he started north, leaving household goods, library, piano, which were never again seen. Carrie his wife and [eight] year old Harriet were bundled into a closed carriage and taken to a station outside the city by friends in his parish. The lines were closed but they had a passport through in Kentucky."

There was a train station in Wilmington a few blocks from their home, but apparently it was thought to be safer if they left from a small rural station. They traveled in a "closed carriage" so no one would see them leaving. Like many people in the world today they were war refugees on a dangerous journey to safety.

I remember my mother telling me this story when I was a child. She said, "When they crossed the border soldiers came onto the train." I don't know whether the soldiers were from the North or the South, but they were checking to see that no one was crossing illegally from the Southern States or bringing war materials in or out.

Aunt Katharine continues the story, "Their trunk was opened; contents scattered, Harriette's doll smashed [to see if papers were hidden in its head], Dr. Wainwright arrested. Carrie protested vigorously, 'Aren't you ashamed to arrest a minister of the Gospel, whose only crime is to comfort the dying and bury the dead whether they wear the blue or the gray?' The guard, who held him by the collar, let him go."

Caroline "Carrie" Hayden Wainwright, aunt/step-mother to Harriet Wainwright. Date unknown.

My mother told me, "Harriet's father was arrested as a spy, but his wife stood up to the soldiers and shamed them so they let him go. But they broke my grandmother's china-headed doll." That was how my mother ended the story. I could see the tears in her eyes and hear the choke in her throat, echoes of her grandmother's grief for her lost doll. Years later, when retelling this story, I feel tears in my eyes. Can you imagine how Harriet must have felt when the soldiers smashed her doll and threatened to imprison her father? But fortunately for all of us, the family story does not end with this sad event.

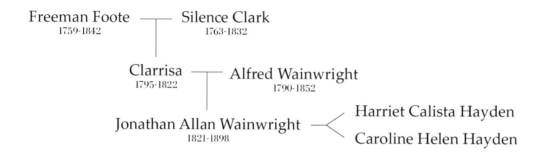

Freeman Foote — Silence Clark
1759-1842   1763-1832

Clarrisa — Alfred Wainwright
1795-1822   1790-1852

Jonathan Allan Wainwright < Harriet Calista Hayden
1821-1898   Caroline Helen Hayden

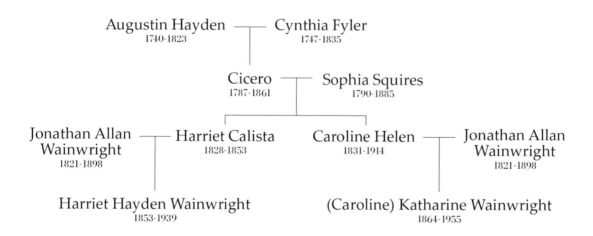

Augustin Hayden — Cynthia Fyler
1740-1823   1747-1835

Cicero — Sophia Squires
1787-1861   1790-1885

Jonathan Allan Wainwright 1821-1898 — Harriet Calista 1828-1853   Caroline Helen 1831-1914 — Jonathan Allan Wainwright 1821-1898

Harriet Hayden Wainwright 1853-1939   (Caroline) Katharine Wainwright 1864-1955

created by Cait Miller

CHAPTER 4

MINISTRY IN CONNECTICUT

I can only speculate, but if the Wainwright family crossed the state line at Cumberland Gap they would have traveled north through the border state of Kentucky along the Wilderness Road built by Daniel Boone and probably passed through Berea where my family settled a century later. I remember the sound of trains, loaded with coal, passing through the tunnel in the Berea ridge and running northward. Now I wonder if it ever occurred to my mother that her grandmother might have passed that same way a hundred years before.

If we follow Aunt Katharine's notes, the family would have changed trains in Cincinnati where years before Jonathan's cousin Harriet Beecher had met and married Calvin Stowe. While the Stowe's lived in the area, Harriet Beecher met many fugitive slaves and collected their stories which she used in writing her book, *Uncle Tom's Cabin*. But by this time the Stowe's had moved on and were living in the north.

Finally the Wainwrights arrived back at the house in Connecticut on Hayden Hill Road. Aunt Katharine writes, "[my father] was commissioned as chaplain of the 19th Regiment CT volunteers, soon after 2nd CT heavy artillery. He was mustered into the service of the US Army, September 10, 1862". The regimental history from Civil War Archives record that this regiment served in Forts Worth and Lyon near Alexandria Virginia, parts of the network of forts protecting Washington, DC. In 1863 they became a heavy artillery unit. Aunt Katharine believed that Jonathan's increasing deafness resulted from this assignment.

Katharine Wainwright
Mackey – half-sister to Harriet
Wainwright. Her scrapbooks form
the basis for this biography.

Jonathan resigned from the army on March 1, 1863. Aunt Katharine writes of her sister," she is running to welcome home this father, Chaplain of the Nineteenth CT Heavy Artillery, who lifts her to the saddle of his spirited black horse - Dandy." She also writes, "Dandy the black stallion war horse was kept for some time after the war. He always stood on his hind feet for a second when starting, just to be friendly. Incidentally fine horses were, next to books a sine qua non[16] in the make-up of this family".

By this time you may be wondering about how Aunt Katharine fits into the family. We have been reading her accounts about her parents, her grandparents, her aunts and uncles and her sister, but we haven't heard anything about her! But in the midst of talking about her father we read this line: "Kitty arrived on the scene May 21, 1864." Like her sister Harriet, Kitty was named for her mother, Caroline in this case. At some point young Caroline Wainwright renamed herself Katharine, with the unusual spelling of two a's, and used the nickname Kitty. A number of members of the Cook branch of the family were named after her and the name has been carried through several generations. My mother was Katharine as are Katharine B. Cook, Kathryn Beilfuss, Laurel Katarina Mylonas-Orwig and Katharine Craig.

After being discharged from the army, the Rev. Jonathan Wainwright became the Rector of St. John's Episcopal Church in Salisbury CT. The church building where he served is still standing although it has had some structural changes since. The bell was added in 1866 during Wainwright's tenure there. The Wainwrights could have put down roots and raised their daughters in the town choosing to remain near their families. Kitty [Aunt Katharine] writes of her visits to the home on Hayden Hill Road, "In my own childhood, one cherished spot was the big pantry where sat the cookie jar, a big cheese and always a supply of pies. Another was the attic, where hung my great-grandfather's (Augustin) uniform, powder horn, and musket – many times my playmates. Then and chiefly, the butternuts with flatiron and hammer handy. Third and looming large in memory were the grafted apples in the cellar."

CHAPTER 5

CALLED TO MOVE WEST

Then Aunt Katharine writes of a visit that brought another train trip for Harriet and her family. "In 1871, Rev. Montgomery Schuyler, Dean of Christ Church Cathedral, St. Louis [MO] was summering at Salisbury, Connecticut, a resort of unusual beauty. With much earnestness he told the Rector of St. John's Church, Rev. Jonathan A. Wainwright, that he was greatly needed in Missouri to uphold St. Paul's College at Palmyra, and to aid in the upbuilding of the church. After due formalities, Dr. Wainwright left his wealthy congregation and started with his wife and two daughters on a three day's journey to Palmyra, passing through Chicago, October tenth, the day after the big fire, while the city was still burning."

In 1871 Chicago was a growing city on Lake Michigan and a railroad hub. The summer had been very dry and on October 8th, high winds fanned flames into a blaze that quickly spread through the wooden buildings. It killed about 300 people and destroyed 17,500 buildings leaving at least 100,000 people homeless. Popular myth says that a cow in the O'Leary barn kicked over a lantern but the exact cause has never been determined. It finally started to rain late on October 9 and the fire ended the next day. Because of the drought and the wind from the south, other serious fires destroyed Peshtigo, Wisconsin, Holland and Manistee, Michigan at the same time.[17]

Palmyra, Missouri is north of St. Louis near the Hannibal home of Samuel Clemens, better known by his pen name, Mark Twain. When you read in Twain's novel, *Tom Sawyer*, about things happening in the county seat, Clemens was referring to Palmyra. The courthouse from that time is still there as is the city jail which fictionally housed the father of Tom Sawyer's friend, Huckleberry Finn.

The college, actually a boys' school, had been built in 1847 and was first called "The Governor Clark Mission."[18] After returning from his expedition to the west coast with Merriweather Lewis, William Clark became the first governor of Missouri. His son, George Rogers Hancock Clark, gave land to the Episcopal Diocese of Missouri with the condition that a mission school be built somewhere in the state. Palmyra was chosen for its site. The school enrolled boarding and day students and as the student body grew, buildings were added to the campus.

> *Missouri was a border state deeply divided by the Civil War. In 1862 the town witnessed the Palmyra Massacre. Andrew Alsman, a Union patriot in an area which favored the Confederacy, helped Union forces arrest local Southern sympathizers. But he was arrested by Confederate Colonel Joseph Porter during a raid. When Porter decided to let him go, Alsman departed the camp and disappeared. Provost Marshal William R. Strachan, representing the Union in control of the area, sent a message to Porter saying that unless Alsman was returned in ten days, ten of Porter's men, who were held as prisoners, would be executed. Likely Alsman was already dead – he was not returned. When the time ran out ten local men who had nothing to do with his disappearance were executed by firing squad. [19]*

During the Civil War, Union troops had used St. Paul College as their base of operations and it was still recovering from damage to its buildings and reputation. Therefore this town would not have been ready to welcome a "Connecticut Yankee" and his outspoken wife! Aunt Katharine recounts the trip, "With Carrie his wife, Hattie (18), Kittie (7), Dr. Wainwright arrived in Chicago, amid the smoldering ruins and devastation of the big fire of Oct. 11, 1871. His oldest sister Mary Webb was living there and they stopped with her family long enough to hear the story of the fire".

"Then Palmyra – a red hot Confederate town in northeast MO, where the effigy of the federal General McNeal – who had ordered ten men shot in reprisal for one man who had mysteriously disappeared – was hung and burned every anniversary. From the station, a mile from the town, the omnibus which held them, swayed from side to side as its occupants clung to their seats. As the door of their room at the National Hotel closed, Carrie flung herself across the bed and sobbing bitterly, begged to go back to Connecticut. The answer was decisive; no return." Eventually they settled in and the students arrived, day pupils and boarding students from St. Louis and elsewhere.

The previous Principal had purchased the school at the end of the Civil War and had "established a wide reputation for managing unruly boys."[20] He had resigned in 1870 and transferred the property to the St. Paul's

College Corporation. The Rev. Mr. Schuyler, who had recruited Wainwright, was on the Board of Trustees. His son, Louis Schuyler, a theological student, was brought in to assist in rebuilding the school.

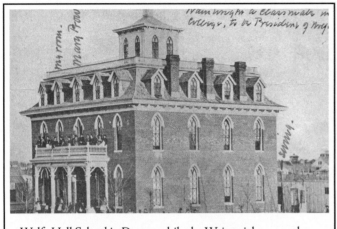

Wolfe Hall School in Denver while the Wainwrights were there.

But this was not to be the last westward move of the family. Aunt Katharine writes: "In 1873, the Rev. John Spaulding, a classmate of Dr. Wainwright in the theological Seminary, who officiated at his wedding, became Bishop of Colorado. He urged his friend to come to Denver for school and missionary work. He went and in the eyes of his wife jumped from the frying pan into the fire. Denver had not a spear of grass, save a fringe along the sidewalks where ditches of mountain water made possible spare cottonwood trees. In his mountain mission work, his buggy had to be anchored to keep it from blowing away. About eleven o'clock every morning, a windstorm sent everyone scurrying to shut doors and window, but even then sand drifted in and had to be cleaned up."

Wolfe Hall was a girls boarding school located in what would become downtown Denver. After Wainwright left, the buildings and land were sold and a new facility was built nearer to St. John's Episcopal Cathedral. The existing Boston Building was later built on the original site of the school. In addition to running the school, Jonathan Wainwright had a parish in Baldswinsville, but this town no longer appears on modern maps. Aunt Katharine writes, "[Harriet] went with her father one Sunday to his Mission at Baldwinsville, some twelve miles from Denver. A rough resort lay midway, over whose gate was the caption 'Whoever enters here is in danger of his life.' On this morning as the two came along in a buggy, a number of men with revolvers pointed toward them, surrounded the buggy. The horse reared and backed. Dr. Wainwright laughed at them and invited them to church. The revolvers were lowered."

Aunt Katharine continues her narrative, "It was a rich missionary field but Carrie with all her fine qualities simply did not possess this kind of zeal. She rebelled, tho' it must be said that Dr. Wainwright took it with saintly acquiescence. She said she would not stay in such Godforsaken country. Beside it, St. Paul's was a paradise. Back they came at the end of a year in the midst of a grasshopper scourge". True to her word, Caroline Hayden Wainwright lived in Palmyra, Missouri until she died in 1914 and is buried in the cemetery at the north end of town next to her husband.

Harriet Wainwright – date unknown.

When the family left Denver Harriet, now 22 years old, was sent back to Connecticut for a New England education. Her sister writes: "Hattie received her music and so on, at Hartford. After leaving Denver, she spent a year among the New England relatives. Here two suitors pressed their claims, but she came home engaged to her cousin, Charles Hayden. The Evans family owes their existence to a change of sentiment."

CHAPTER 5

HARRIET'S MARRIAGE

Jonathan Wainwright returned to Palmyra as principal of St. Paul's school and priest for the local Episcopal parish. In 1877 the school was sold by the Diocese of St. Louis at auction and Wainwright bought it for $5359.[21] He made it a coeducational school. Aunt Katharine writes that by 1878 it was "crowded beyond its capacity with thirty-two boarding pupils and a large day attendance. With a faculty of high grade teachers, the school at this time reached numerically its highest peak of success."

This is the farmhouse in Wales where John Evans lived and where seven of his brothers and sisters were born.

One of the teachers at the school was young John Evans. He was born in Wales in 1842 into a family of farmers who worked on rented land. John had nine brothers and sisters. He was educated at Swansea University, equivalent of a high school in those days, and finished a theological course at Lampeter University, Wales in 1865. My mother told me that as a young child her Grandfather John had fallen into a fire and his hands were so badly scarred and deformed that he had trouble holding anything. He usually wore gloves to cover the scars. In 1866 he opened a school in Llanelly, Wales "for the education of Boys in Latin, Greek, French, Algebra, Arithmetic, Euclid Measuration, the Elements of Chemistry and Natural Philosophy; English, including Writing, Reading,

Grammar, and Composition; History, Geography, and &c." The school was held in a room adjoining Llanelly Church but was "strictly undenominational". [22]

In 1871 his family decided it was time to leave Wales and find a better life in America. They traveled across the Atlantic and settled near Hiawatha, Kansas, probably in the Welsh community of Padonia, trading the long coast and mountains for the rolling prairie of Kansas. By that time one of John's brothers had died and was buried in Wales. Soon after their trip, one of John's sisters returned to Wales. There she got married and inherited all the family furniture. [23]

One of the challenges of finding the family story involves research. The Internet has made it easier to find long-lost relatives. Thanks to some genealogy sites, I found Tanya Evans Ryle, another descendant of Harriet's, living in Arizona and she connected me with John's great-grandniece Ann Phillips, who was the great-great-granddaughter of the sister who went back to Wales. Bill and I visited her and her husband several years ago in Wales and she showed me where the Evans family had lived, the churches they had attended, and Lampeter College including the chapel where John would have worshiped as a student. As far as I can tell, there aren't any Evans relatives left in Kansas. Another Evans family with similar names settled there about the same time so tracing them is difficult. Except for Ann, we have lost track of all the descendants of John's brothers and sisters. But several of us have DNA registered with the Ancestry site and hope that this may lead to some of these lost cousins.

John Evans – date unknown.

One of John Evan's obituaries states, "…he taught school until 1874, and then came to the United States with his father, who took up a homestead claim near Hiawatha, Kansas. He still continued to teach, finally taking a chair in Park College, Parkville, MO. From there he went to the Episcopal Theological seminary at Nashota, WI, where he studied for a year."[24]

Aunt Katharine writes: "On July 4, 1879, Mr. John Evans, originally from Llanelli, Wales, a graduate of St. David's College [Lampeter] and the University of Swansea, came to St. Paul's for a year of teaching and his final examinations for Deacon's Orders under Dr. Wainwright, who was the Examining Chaplain of the Diocese of Missouri. He taught English and was the headmaster of the Preparatory Department. He proved to be an instructor of very unusual merit and remained three years. He was then ordained deacon by Bishop Robertson in the stone chapel on the College grounds and for a while had charge of St. Jude's church at Monroe City, Missouri."

By the time John Evans arrived in Palmyra, Harriet was twenty five and still unmarried. Like John she was a teacher at St. Paul school. Her sister writes, "A very exceptional teacher, Mr. Evans was greatly beloved and his rich voice in native Welsh songs was a never ending delight. It was quite the natural thing that he and Harriette should be drawn together." She also mentions that he had serious eye trouble and Hattie helped to entertain him during this time.

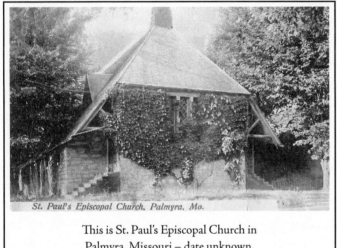

St. Paul's Episcopal Church, Palmyra, Mo.

This is St. Paul's Episcopal Church in Palmyra, Missouri – date unknown.

At about the time of John Evans' arrival at the school, plans were being made to replace the chapel building on the school grounds. Since Jonathan Wainwright was also the rector of the Episcopal congregation that worshiped there, he concluded that the new building should be built close to the center of Palmyra for the convenience of the members. Some of the building materials would be taken from the original chapel. In addition Aunt Katharine writes that Jonathan "gathered over a thousand dollars from his former parishioners at Salisbury.... On June 8, 1880, [John Evans] was ordained Deacon at the last service held in the Gothic chapel in the College grounds and in his first surplice walked with seven clergymen and a large concourse of people, behind Bishop Robertson of Missouri and Bishop Burgess of Quincy Diocese to the laying of the cornerstone of a new church." John Evans first served St. Jude's church at Monroe City, Missouri, but soon became an assistant at Trinity Episcopal Church in Alpena, Michigan.

On October 26, 1882 the Rev. John Evans returned to Palmyra to marry Harriet Wainwright. A newspaper account of their wedding, probably written by her sister Katharine, announces "Thursday evening the marriage of Miss Hattie Wainwright and Rev. John Evans was solemnized in this city by Rev. Ethelbert Talbot of Macon City at St. Paul's church." Talbot had been a teacher of German, Latin and mathematics at St. Paul's college. Continuing the description, "The wedding though a quiet one was elegant in the extreme....At three o'clock the minister in his flowing white robes entered the chancel. He knelt and rose and the groom, in English fashion, came from the vestry and with his 'best man' Rev. Robert Talbot, awaited the coming of the bride at the altar. The moment was at hand, for the ushers passed a white ribbon across the entrance of the pews – an innocent sign of restraint for that gentle company – the organ poured out the wedding march, and with the slow and measured step the ushers passed up the aisle. Close behind, preceded by her attendant [her sister Katharine], came the bride leaning upon the arm of her father, who performed that part of the church service of giving the bride away. The bridal party remained at the altar during the singing of Dank's *'Gloria'* and left the church to the notes of *The Grand March from Tannhauser."* The clipping is too worn to read at this point but another account says that the bride was attired "in a handsome traveling costume of garnet color and plush, with bonnet to match, trimmed with long drooping plume and Mousquetaire gloves".[25]

CHAPTER 6

A CLERGYMAN'S WIFE

John Wainwright Evans taken in Alpena, Michigan in 1883.

Following the wedding, John took his wife back to Alpena, Michigan. Her sister wrote, "Now begins the varied and strenuous life of a clergyman's wife." Alpena had been founded in 1853 as a fishing village along the northeast coast of the lower peninsula of Michigan. When Harriet and John settled there it was a sawmill town in the middle of a prime timbering area. In addition to assisting at Trinity Church in Alpena, The Rev. Evans had charge of Grace Episcopal Church in nearby Long Rapids. The history of Long Rapids Township says that the church was founded in 1882, presumably by John Evans.[26] Their son, John Wainwright, was born in October 1883 in Alpena.

Two years later the family move to Au Sable, Michigan, another lumbering center. Their daughter, Gertrude Sophia, was born there in 1885. Like many lumber towns across the pine woods of Michigan, Wisconsin and Minnesota, it was subject to fires and in 1911 a fire destroyed the county seat and my grandmother's birth certificate, which may be part of the reason she never traveled abroad.

In 1889 John Evans became an assistant at St. George's church in Detroit. Aunt Katharine writes of his time in Michigan that he "was especially fruitful in establishing and erecting churches and parish houses."

She writes of his subsequent moves, "He was ordained to the priesthood by Bishop Coxe of Western New York (1890) and served in his diocese of Clyde and

Gertrude Sophia Evans age 3

Youngstown for a number of years." A clipping from the Clyde New York *Times Newspaper* says: "At the farewell reception given Mr. Evans and family at St. John's rectory, Tuesday, Dec. 22, 1891, the following resolutions …were unanimously adopted: Whereas, Our rector, Rev. John Evans, came to this parish an entire stranger, and by his discreet, upright and Christian example, has won the affectionate regard of the members of the parish and the esteem of the whole community, and Whereas, after a useful and honorable service of two years and three months in Clyde, he has deemed it expedient to accept a call elsewhere, which gives promise for him of a wider field of usefulness and prosperity; therefore, Resolved, by the wardens and vestrymen of St. John's church that it is with feelings of most sincere regret we part with our beloved rector, Rev. John Evans. Combining true manhood with Christian living, he has been faithful to every duty and has done all in his power to promote the spiritual as well as the temporal welfare of this parish. Resolved, that, while this parting is one of sorrow to all, we extend to Mr. Evans and his devoted and estimable wife, our heartfelt congratulations on the prospect for their increased prosperity; and we trust they will always find in their new parish as true and sincere friends as those they leave behind them in Clyde."

On November 22, 1891 The Rev. John Evans began his ministry in Youngstown, New York. John Evans' son John Wainwright, known in family as Wain, wrote in 1967 of his boyhood in Youngstown, "I could write a book about Youngstown and my memories of it." Wain and Gertrude went to the district school with four grades in each room. Youngstown was a fishing town across the Niagara River from Canada. Uncle Wain writes that his father used to cross the river to visit the Anglican rector in Niagara-on-the-Lake, Ontario. "One day when I went along, Papa and I stopped at a restaurant with a bar and had something to eat. And he ordered a glass of beer taking his chance that someone would recognize him from the other side. Of course beer in that Canadian town was perfectly respectable. [but it was not respectable for ministers in Youngstown!]. Anyway, he had his beer, and I get pleasure from the memory of it to this day. It makes me realize how little I knew about my father. Instinctively I realized that, in a very small way, he had gone on a spree and beaten the devil around the stump. It was his wild oat. I never peeped about it in Youngstown, even to my mother." He also comments that "my father had no hands". I never thought to have my mother describe the extent of his injuries from accidental burning as a child, but she thought this was one reason they moved so often – some people in each congregation were squeamish about his scarred and deformed fingers.

John's father, David Evans, died March 8, 1891 and was buried in Hiawatha, KS. His mother died September 7, 1892. John wrote the obituary for his mother in Welsh and said they "were members of the Baptist Church and were 'brought into the fold' at Sardis [Chapel] Llanedi during their youth. Their faith was pure, sincere and unshakeable. [or words to that effect!] " I am the Resurrection and the Life," said The Lord, "They who believe in me, though they may die, yet may they live" J.E. [presumably her son John Evans]. This was translated by our Welsh cousin, Ann Philips.[27]

Sardis Chapel in Wales

In 1895 the Evans family moved to Monroe, Michigan where he was instrumental in building a handsome Rectory at Trinity Episcopal Church. The Rectory and the Church are still standing. I was able to visit them during a long layover at the Detroit airport a number of years ago.

Meanwhile, Jonathan Wainwright's deafness had made it necessary for him to give up teaching. In 1886 St. Paul's college became a girls' school under the management of Katharine Wainwright, whose specialty was music. But eventually Katharine developed health problems which forced the closing of the school. In 1896 she married Warren Mackey of Palmyra at St. Paul's and became stepmother to his two children. He built her a lovely house which she named "Highdown" the original spelling of the Haydon name. They never had any children of their own, but she remained close to Harriet's children and grandchildren and corresponded regularly with them. When my mother took me to meet her as a child of five or so, she gave me two peacock feathers and a necklace of pink beads which I had restrung and passed along to Kathryn Beilfuss Wall when she was married.

Jonathan continued to serve as the Rector of the church in Palmyra until his death on November 15, 1898. The pulpit at the church was given in his honor by his daughters and the lectern was given in memory of his first wife, Harriet Hayden, by her sister, Caroline, his second wife. Recently the church was sold and the lectern was taken to the Episcopal Church in Hannibal, but the pulpit was too large to move. The Rt. Rev. Daniel Tuttle, Bishop of Missouri, spoke of Wainwright at his funeral, "I am sad to lose him. Dear faithful cheery soul! He was afflicted with almost entire deafness, yet he sturdily and steadily worked on into his 78th year. He kept to the writing of new sermons. He studied new books, he was in touch with the thought and activities of the day. It was a great inspiration to me to be with him, and see how the noble spirit disdained to be hampered by the trammels of the flesh. I learned much from him and was helped much by him. It is sadness to me to know I am to see him no more in the Church Militant. But it is gladness to feel that it is peace and rest and love and Home for him. He was a faithful soldier and servant." [28]

Jonathan Wainwright – date unknown

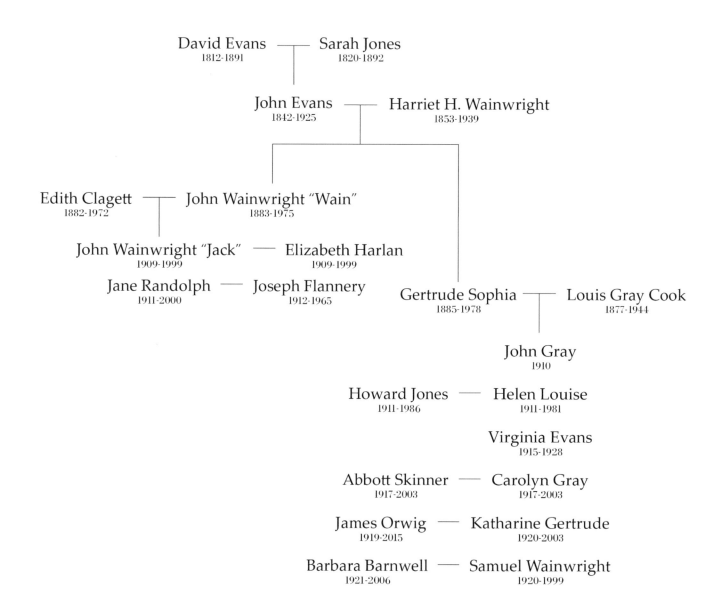

David Evans
1812-1891
— Sarah Jones
1820-1892

John Evans
1842-1925
— Harriet H. Wainwright
1853-1939

Edith Clagett
1882-1972
— John Wainwright "Wain"
1883-1975

John Wainwright "Jack"
1909-1999
— Elizabeth Harlan
1909-1999

Jane Randolph
1911-2000
— Joseph Flannery
1912-1965

Gertrude Sophia
1885-1978
— Louis Gray Cook
1877-1944

John Gray
1910

Howard Jones
1911-1986
— Helen Louise
1911-1981

Virginia Evans
1915-1928

Abbott Skinner
1917-2003
— Carolyn Gray
1917-2003

James Orwig
1919-2015
— Katharine Gertrude
1920-2003

Barbara Barnwell
1921-2006
— Samuel Wainwright
1920-1999

CHAPTER 7

FRONTIER MINISTRY

In 1901 Harriet and her family were off to the frontier again, this time to Miles City, Montana. The Emmanuel Episcopal Church in Miles City is one of the oldest in the state and the building John Evans knew is still standing. The congregation was founded in 1881 as St. Paul's church. The name was changed in 1887 when Emmanuel Episcopal Church in Baltimore, Maryland made a substantial donation to the construction of the current building.[29] Just to show that we never know much our family history can influence our own lives consider this: John Evans' great-granddaughter, The Rev. Anne Orwig Weatherholt, her husband, the Rev. Allan Weatherholt, and her daughter-in-law, the Rev. Elizabeth Sipos, are priest in the Diocese of Maryland, where Emmanuel Episcopal Church is located. Elizabeth moved to the United States from Canada where she served a church in Niagara, Ontario near Youngstown, New York. Anne's son, Daniel, is a Church organist and administrator, also in the Diocese of Maryland.

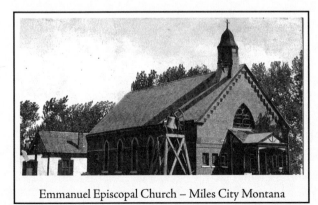
Emmanuel Episcopal Church – Miles City Montana

Aunt Katharine writes about John Evans: "In Miles City he again left the story of his work in building missionary churches. When St. Paul's church at Palmyra was refurnished, the pulpit and other furnishings were sent to a new church he had completed at Rosebud, Montana, one of his mission locations." The church in Rosebud is still standing and is now Rosebud Community Church. In 2007 it was put on the National Register of Historic Places. The application papers tell about its history:"In 1896, Fred and

Mary Mefford arrived in Rosebud from the Midwest and rallied support for a local Episcopal congregation." Later in the article it mentions that the Meffords came from St. Jude's Church in Monroe City, Missouri which had been John Evans' first parish. The application paper explains, "Episcopalian missionary bishops established missionary districts, and identified communities from which to base their evangelical practice…. This was the case at Rosebud, Montana, where the nascent congregation benefitted from the church at Miles City. Rosebud was, at that time, a budding agricultural community along the Northern Pacific Railroad line." The article says that the church was built with volunteer labor in 1906 under the direction of a local carpenter named Alfred Drescher. It mentions that "Emmanuel Episcopal Church in Miles City donated the pews," but I wonder if they were part of the furnishings that came from St. Paul's in Palmyra. [30]

Mission Church in Rosebud, Montana.

In 1903, while the Evans family was living in Miles City, their son, John Wainwright entered Princeton. During his college years he was a correspondent for the *New York Times* and the *Philadelphia Inquirer*. In a short biography Aunt Katharine writes, "in 1907, he acted a private detective in Drummond Agency, New York; in the City News Association, covered the Coroner's Office in the old Criminal Courts building; was transferred to the covering of banks during the beginnings of the 1907 Panic, and was press agent of the Lakewood Hotel, Lakewood, New Jersey, thru winter season. In May, 1908, became reporter of the *New York Herald*."

John Wainwright, known to the family as Wain, married Edith Claggett of Palmyra on July 9, 1908. Aunt Katharine records that Edith was the daughter of Jennie Anderson and the Rev. William H. Claggett, a Presbyterian minister. Her grandfather was Colonel Thomas Lilbourne Anderson, "a lawyer of statewide reputation in Missouri; member of congress during Buchanan's incumbency. In his home at Palmyra, she was reared after the early death of her mother." Katharine's records say that through his mother Colonel Anderson was descended from the prominent Randolph family of Virginia. Anderson's grandfather had been a captain in Washington's army during the Revolutionary War. His obituary describes Anderson as "a friend of the oppressed; a lover of liberty and justice; an advanced thinker, a patriot, statesman and a Christian." Wain and Edith had planned to marry in Palmyra but were wed in Philadelphia where her father was taking care of her stepmother. Edith had a degree in Literature from the University of Texas and did two years of graduate work at Bryn Mawr College before becoming a high school teacher in Port Arthur, Texas before her wedding.[31]

Colonel Thomas Anderson,
Edith Claggett's grandfather.

Aunt Katharine writes that Wain and Edith had a son, John Wainwright Evans, Jr., born on May 14, 1909 in New York City and known as "Jack". Their daughter, Jane Randolph Evans was born, January 16, 1911 while the family was living in Palmyra and Wain was "doing fiction and reporting for the St. Louis *Globe Democrat*." The following years "were spent in teaching – Mathematics at Smith Academy, St. Louis, Mo; English at the University of Arkansas, three years; Journalism at the University of Kansas, two years; and during two summers, Journalism at the University of Wisconsin. In the fall of 1917, became assistant editor for The Nation's Business, Washington, D.C., specializing in article work. In 1919, participated in a campaign in New York City, to raise twelve million dollars for the Salvation Army."

CHAPTER 8

LAST YEARS

Emily Gray and Samuel Cook, parents of Louis Cook.

Gertrude also left for college from Miles City. It was unusual for women to go to college at that time and the nearest college was the University of Minnesota where she enrolled with a girlfriend. Her Aunt Katharine writes: "In her sophomore year, boarding in Prospect Park, she met Louis Cook at a church gathering – his first year of teaching at East High School."

Louis had been born in 1877 in Kalamazoo, Michigan. His parents were Samuel Clemens Cook and Emily Gray of Dexter, Michigan. Louis' ancestors had come from New York State and settled in Dexter before Michigan had become a state. Aunt Katharine knew that Gertrude's ancestors had been on the sailing ship Mary & John in 1630, but she would have been pleased to know that some of Emily Gray's ancestors had also been on that ship and had also settled in Windsor, Connecticut. Louis' father, Samuel, worked for St. Paul Harvester Works and settled in Minneapolis in 1886. The Cook family moved into a house in the recently developed Prospect Park at 56 Clarence Avenue, just south of the water tower at the top of the hill overlooking the Mississippi River and the campus of the University. The house still exists. Louis attended the University of Minnesota and became a teacher and then a principal. After Gertrude graduated she taught for two years in Hutchinson, Minnesota.

Several rectors followed Wainwright's tenure at St. Paul's and in 1907 the Rev. John Evans, Wainwright's son-in-law, was called Wainwright's son-in-law - was called to the church in Palmyra. Two years after John and Harriet returned to Palmyra, Louis and Gertrude were married at St. Paul's. The newly-weds moved into the family house on Clarence Avenue joining his parents while Louis continued to teach at East High in Minneapolis. The high school was on University Avenue and was torn down in 1950 to make room for a shopping center.

Samuel Cook died in 1910. His funeral was held at St. Timothy Episcopal Church which Emily Cook had arranged to have built near her home in Prospect Park. The building is still there and has been used by various groups over time. Emily Gray Cook, Louis' mother, died in March 1920 while visiting relatives in Sherman, Texas. Aunt Katharine Mackey remembered her as "a person of strong convictions and personality, a staunch Episcopalian, an ardent Democrat. She left her impress."[32]

In 1912 John and Harriet moved to Minneapolis to be near Gertrude and her growing family. John served as Assistant Priest at Gethsemane Episcopal Church which is still open and in use in downtown Minneapolis. They lived for several years in the house on Clarence Avenue. All six of Gertrude and Louis' children were born in that house. The first, a boy named John Gray, died soon after birth in 1910, two weeks after the death of his grandfather Samuel Cook. Helen Louise was born in July 1911. Virginia Evans was born in February 1915. As a child she caught rheumatic fever which weakened her heart. At that time there was no heart surgery so she was always an invalid and died at age 13. Carolyn Gray was born in 1917 and the twins Katharine Gertrude and Samuel Wainwright arrived in 1920.

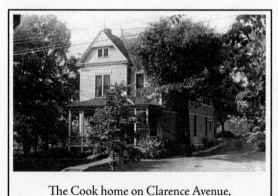

The Cook home on Clarence Avenue,
Minneapolis, Minnesota

In 1914 John and Harriet moved to Wabasha, Minnesota where he served as Rector of Grace Memorial Episcopal Church, one of the oldest Episcopal churches in the state. The building is still there and is known for its Cass Gilbert architecture and Tiffany window. Aunt Katharine called the church Trinity, but it is clearly the same structure as Grace. He retired from ministry in March 1917 and returned to Minneapolis.

In November of 1920 John Evans wrote in a letter to his niece in Wales, "We are making a change for the winter. Mr. Cook, Gertrude's husband has gone to Great Falls, Montana where he is principal of the high school. It is 1000 miles North West of here. We will come back here in the spring, I mean, Hattie and I. We must see them located safely. The stork has brought Gertrude twins, Oct. 1st, a boy and a girl. Hence the necessity of our helping out in the moving." In

February 1921 he wrote to his niece from Great Falls, "Hattie and I expect to come to see you all next summer…I want to be in Wales during summer weather for I know you have much rain in the winter."

In 1922 Louis Cook accepted the job of principal of the new high school being built in Northeast Minneapolis. When he was hired he was allowed to name the school and picked the name Edison. The school is still in use in 2018. In those days Northeast Minneapolis was an immigrant community made up of Scandinavians and Eastern Europeans. It continues to be an immigrant community populated with Africans, Hispanics and Asians. The Cooks lived at 2402 Johnson Street across from Windom Park in NE Minneapolis. All of their children graduated from Edison High School. Each year the Louis Cook Scholarship is awarded to an outstanding senior. Several times Louis' grandson, Stephen Cook, has been present to make the award. Another grandson, Robert Skinner, has done volunteer work there and recently a great-grandson, William Louis Craig, worked there to update the auditorium where Louis Cook had once led student assemblies.

In April of 1922, the Rev. John Evans wrote from the Clarence Avenue house, "When I wrote to you last time I was contemplating making a trip to Wales but that war threw cold water over it and according to the advice of Cousin John of Llanwrtyd I gave it up." Apparently this is referring to the after effects of WWI and Cousin John thought that John Evans at 79 was too old for such a trip. John Evans never returned to Wales. Some years ago, after my trip to Wales and visit with Cousin Ann Philips, I slipped a cobble from a Welsh beach under a corner of his tombstone. John continued his letter, "My children are 39 and 37, Wainwright and Gertrude respectively. Wain, as we call him for short, lives in New York and writes for magazines. Gertrude, whose married name is Cook, lives in Minnesota. They have five children Helen, Virginia, Carolyn, Samuel, Katharine. …Wain has two children, John Wainwright and Jane Randolph. …I expect to live at least another ten years. I am well and strong and I preach almost every Sunday. …I am retired, as it is called here, and receive a pension from the church."

Despite his optimistic predictions, the Rev. John Evans died February 9, 1925 at St. Barnabas Hospital in Minneapolis. The funeral was held at St. Timothy Church in Prospect Park, Minneapolis, Minnesota. He was buried in Lakewood Cemetery, (section 19, plot 8) near the Cook plot. His sister-in-law, Aunt Katharine Mackey, wrote his obituary for the Palmyra paper, "Through forty-four years of devoted service in the work of the Master and the church, Mr. Evans has battled against odds quite

Evans family – about 1923, Front: Virginia and Carolyn Cook, Middle: J. Wainwright, Harriet and John Evans, Katharine, Gertrude and Samuel Cook, Back: Jane, Edith and John W. Evans, Louis and Helen Cook.

out of the ordinary. His wife has fully shared this burden and together they have won without exception, the love and esteem of their parishioners. Mr. Evans has earned the fullness of joy which is now his."

Harriet Wainwright Evans, now a widow, moved in with the Cooks on Johnson Street and watched her grandchildren grow. She died February 26, 1939. Her sister Aunt Katharine Mackey wrote her obituary, and I have used many quotes from it for this story. She closes by saying, "The outstanding fulfillment of Harriet Evans life lies in her two children, Wainwright Evans of NYC, who fights with his pen for tolerance and sane thinking; Gertrude Cook, who stands solidly back of her husband in leading thousands of boys and girls in nobility of character at Edison High School in Minneapolis. Also her grandchildren, John W. Evans, at the head of the Astronomical Observatory at Mills College near San Francisco; Jane Evans Flannery, now residing with her husband in India; Helen Cook Jones, with her husband at Yale University, who presented her with two great grandchildren, Richard and Harriet; Carolyn, Katharine, and Sam Cook, students at the Minnesota University. These are the high spots in the life …. of a three pound baby who thru eighty-five years, met life with splendid fortitude."

When I started this project I thought that it was the book that should have been written by Aunt Katharine, Harriet's half-sister, or by my mother who had heard her stories as a child. But because I have access to the Internet I have been able to add to the stories in ways that would have been impossible for them. The Internet led me to cousins Ann Philips and Tanya Ryle and more recently, Mike Flannery who shared their information with me. I have used the Internet to reach out to the various churches where Jonathan and John served, to gather additional information to flesh out the story.

I have always felt that the story of the escape from North Carolina needed to be told, but it always ended so abruptly and tearfully with the broken doll. Now I can tell you that story and what happened next. Because of Harriet's adventurous life, we have our lives and can pass these stories on to the next generations.

Dick Jones and Harriet Rechnitz are the only family members still alive who met Harriet Wainwright Evans and they were very young. But many of us knew her grandchildren and can connect to her through them. I have asked my cousins to write about Harriet's grandchildren and their children so you can find the names of your parents and grandparents and figure out how you are part of Harriet's on-going story.

CHAPTER 9

HARRIET'S FAMILY

J. Wainwright and Edith Evans contributed by their grandson, Michael Flannery

In the '50s and '60's John Wainwright and Edith Evans lived in West Nyack, New York. Wainwright was a writer for magazines and wrote on a full range of subjects from bee keeping to the paranormal. He also wrote several books about the philosophy of Judge Ben B. Lindsey who presided over a family court in Denver in the 1920s (*The Revolt of Modern Youth*, and *The Companionate Marriage*). In the 1960s they moved to La Luz, New Mexico to be near their son, John who was the director of Sunspot Lunar Observatory (over 10,000 ft in elevation in the mountains above Alamogordo, New Mexico). Edith Clagget Evans died on May 7, 1972 and John Wainwright Evans died on November 30, 1975.

John Wainwright Evans – contributed by his great-granddaughter Tanya Ryle

John W. Evans, first son of J. Wainwright and Edith Evans was born in 1909 and called Jack. He married Elizabeth Harlan after he graduated from Swarthmore College. He earned a doctorate in astrophysics from Harvard and taught for several years. During WWII he worked on special optical systems for military use. After the war he worked at several observatories ending as director of the Sacramento Peak Observatory in New Mexico where he helped design a solar telescope. Their three children were Wainwright (Wain), Nancy Jane and Jeanne. After retirement they lived in Santa Fe, New Mexico. Jack and Betty both died in 1999.

Jane Randolph Evans contributed by her son, Mike Flannery

Jane Randolph Evans was born in 1911. Jane graduated from Oberlin College in Ohio, and moved to New York City during the Depression. She was a beautiful dancer and taught ballroom dancing at Arthur Murray Dance studio, where she met Joseph Howard Flannery. They quickly fell in love, but unfortunately Joe worked for an International trading company which sent him to Ceylon soon after they met. She followed him out there six months later on a six week voyage by freighter to Colombo, Ceylon. They married the day the shipped docked, 19 December 1937. They had three children-Gale, born in Calcutta, India, Michael born in Washington DC,, and Carol, born in Johannesburg, South Africa. Joe and Jane finally moved back to the USA in the mid-1960s. Joe died in 1965, and Jane in 2000.

Gertrude Evans Cook

At each meal the Cook family blessed the food with what we call the "Cook Family Prayer" which we still use at family gatherings: "Bless, O Lord, this portion of Your bounty to our use and comfort, and ourselves to Thy loving service, for Jesus' sake. Amen." God has continued to bless this family and they have remained faithful to the call to service. All their children and their spouses and all their grandchildren and their spouses chose careers of service to others in the fields of ministry, education, medicine, social work, public service and fine arts. Most of their great grandchildren are continuing in these fields.

Louis Cook died suddenly on March 30, 1944. Gertrude continued living in the house on Johnson Street and converted the upstairs to a separate apartment which she rented to students at nearby Bethel College. She eventually moved to the Episcopal Church home in St. Paul and lived there independently yet involved with the families of Sam and Carolyn and visited by the families of Helen and Katharine. Gertrude died on February 13, 1978.

Helen Cook Jones contributed by daughter Harriet Jones Rechnitz

Helen Louise Cook met Howard Robert Jones while they were both students at the University of Minnesota. After graduating, Howard began his career as a teacher and counselor in Minneapolis. Helen and Howard were married on December 27, 1934 in a ceremony at St. Mark's Episcopal Church in Minneapolis. Daughter Harriet Louise and son Richard Howard (Dick) were born in St. Paul. In 1938 the family moved east to New Haven where Howard studied for his Ph.D. Degree at Yale University. Howard then held several academic and administrative positions in New England. A third child, Virginia Cook (Ginny) was born in New Canaan, CT. At age 34, Howard accepted the position of president of Plymouth Teachers College in Plymouth, New Hampshire. Howard instituted considerable change in the college administration and curriculum, Helen modernized the stately president's house. In 1951, the family moved to Ann Arbor, Michigan where Howard served as professor and chairman of Educational Administration at the University of Michigan. After the children were grown, Helen earned a M.A. Degree of Arts in Library Science from the University of Michigan. In yet another move (1963), Howard became Dean of the College of Education at the University of Iowa. Helen was hired as library/media specialist at Grant Woods Elementary School. Helen and Howard spent the remainder of their lives in Iowa City, but traveled extensively. Helen died in 1981, and Howard in 1986.

Carolyn Cook Skinner contributed by daughter Susan Skinner Beilfuss

Carolyn graduated from the University of Minnesota with a Home Economics degree and a teaching license. Her first teaching job was in Zumbrota MN. Carolyn was a bridesmaid when Helen married Howard Jones and she met Abbott Skinner who was a groomsman. She married Abbott in 1940 and moved to Boston where he graduated from Harvard Medical School and then served as a doctor in WWII. Carolyn loved cooking, sewing, playing Bridge and reading. She was active in church and did many volunteer jobs. They had four children, Charles Abbott, Thomas Harvey, Susan Carol and Robert Wain. The family lived in the Highland Park neighborhood of St. Paul and enjoyed "going to the cabin" on Blue Lake near Zimmerman, MN. They traveled abroad to Europe, Asia and Africa. They were a perfect couple and were always in love. Carolyn died in 2003, two months before Abbott. They are buried in the Skinner plot in Roselawn Cemetery, St. Paul.

Summary of Katharine Cook contributed by daughter Peg Craig

Katharine Cook met James Orwig at Camp Miniwanca, a Christian leadership camp, in Michigan where she was spending the summer helping her sister Helen with her two small children while Howard worked at the camp. Katharine and her brother Sam enrolled in the college conference of the camp and attended four years. Katharine and Jim were married at the camp on June 27, 1943 with Carolyn as Maid of Honor and Sam as Best Man. Jim was on leave from the army, he went to Italy with the 10th Mountain Division during World War II. After studying at The University of Wisconsin and Michigan State University, Jim Orwig became Dean of Men at Berea College in KY in 1955. They had daughters Margaret Evans (Peg), Elizabeth Forbes (Betsy) and Anne Louise. Katharine had taught science before her marriage but while in Berea served in many volunteer roles in church and community. After retirement they spent a year serving as missionaries in Hong Kong and two years in Chiang Mai, Thailand. Katharine died on October 10, 2003 and Jim on January 9, 2015.

Summary of Samuel Cook contributed by son Steve Cook

During World War II Sam served in the Navy with the rank of Lt JG. He was a part of the Normandy Invasion landing at Omaha Beach after commanding a landing craft that ferried supplies between ships. It was only after the invasion, and the cloak of silence lifted for the preparations, that Sam learned that his father, Louis, had died several months earlier. It was during his time in the Service that Sam decided to pursue the ministry. Near the end of the war Sam met Barbara Barnwell and they married on April 6th, 1946. Sam enrolled in Seabury Western Seminary in Evanston, Illinois . Their first child Stephen was born there in 1949. Soon afterwards the family moved to Minnetonka Beach, Minnesota where Sam began his Parish work at St. Martins. During his service there, Kathy, in 1950 and David, in 1951 were born. Margaret was born in 1954 and died shortly after birth. Sam would later have Parishes at St. Mary's in St. Paul and Calvary in Rochester. It was while at St. Mary's that Sam was granted a Scholarship for advanced degree study abroad in Canterbury, England in 1958. Upon returning to St. Mary's, Betsy was born in 1961. Following retirement Sam and Barbara moved to Traverse City, Michigan where they could be by Kathy and her family. He died there on November 22, 1999. Barbara died on September 2, 2006. They are buried at Lakewood Cemetery, Minneapolis.

ENDNOTES

1 The Foote History and Genealogy by by Abram William Foote. Clarissa's name is spelled with one r and two s's in Foote's book but her tombstone uses two r's and one s so that is how I have it in the family tree.

2 https://en.wikipedia.org/wiki/ /Uncle_Tom%27s_Cabin

3 https://en.wikipedia.org/wiki/Harriet_Beecher_Stowe

4 The Foote History and Genealogy by Abram William Foote

5 Katharine W. Mackey scrapbooks

6 https://en.wikipedia.org/wiki/French_and_Indian_War

7 https://windsorhistoricalsociety.org/faq-items/augustin-haydens-french-and-indian-war-journals/

8 https://en.wikipedia.org/wiki/George_Howe,_3rd_Viscount_Howe

9 https://en.wikipedia.org/wiki/Israel_Putnam

10 Records of the Connecticut line of the Hayden family by Jabez Haskell Hayden 1888.

11 Katharine Mackey's scrapbooks

12 History of St. John's Episcopal, Wilmington, NC

13 When John Noble died in 1773 in Danbury, CT he "gives to his daughter Rachel his Negro man Robbin." Since Noble is an ancestor of Louis Cook, this does not apply to the cousins on the Evans branch, but Edith Claggett was a descendant of the Randolph family of Virginia so it is likely that they also had slaves.

14 History of St. John's Episcopal, Wilmington, NC

15 Alice Brooks, Wilmington, NC

16 Means "essential thing".

17 https://en.wikipedia.org/wiki/Great_Chicago_Fire

18 Katharine Mackey's scrapbooks

19 https://en.wikipedia.org/wiki/Palmyra_massacre

20 Tales of the College Yard, by Katharine W. Mackey (1931)

21 Tales of the College Yard, by Katharine W. Mackey (1931)

22 Katharine Mackey's scrapbooks

23 This information is from our Welsh cousin, Ann Philips. She now has the furniture passed down from her great-grandmother.

24 Katharine Mackey's scrapbooks

25 Katharine Mackey's scrapbooks

26 http://www.longrapidstownship.org/?s=grace

27 Evans – Medi 7, 1892, yn Hiawatha,Kansas, yn 76 mlwydd oed, Mrs. Sarah Evans, gweddw David Evans er s blwyddyn a haner. Daethant i'r wlad hon i Hiawatha yn 1871 o Llanedi, Sir Gaerfyrddin Cymru. Bu iddynt ddeg o blant, pump o fechgyn a phump o ferched, saith o honynt yn awr yn fyw, a'r oil yn briod ond un. Y tad a'r fam oeddynt yn aeiodau o eglwys y Bedyddwyr, wedi eu aerbyn yn Sardis, Llanedi, pan yn en hieuenctid. Yr oed en crefydd yn bur, d halog a difrycheulyd. "Myfi yw'r adgyiodiad a'r bywyd, medd yr Arg…dd; yr hwn sydd yn credu ynof fi sr iado …JE

28 Katharine Mackey's scrapbooks

29 https://www.episcopalchurch.org/parish/emmanuel-episcopal-church-miles-city-mt

30 https://catalog.archives.gov/id/71976558

31 Katharine Mackey's scrapbooks

32 When I was researching her ancestry I came across this story which was too amazing to leave out. One of Emily's grandmothers was Betsey Read Tyler Gray. Betsey's brother, Joseph Tyler had a son named Columbus Tyler. Columbus married a woman named Mary Sawyer. When Mary was a young girl she sat up all night nursing a newborn lamb who had been found nearly dead. The lamb recovered and one day she took it to school. Their seats were enclosed in some way to keep the students out of drafts and Mary put the lamb at her feet on her shawl. When she was called to the front of the classroom to recite, the lamb followed her. The teacher laughed and the students giggled, but Mary was embarrassed and led the lamb out to a nearby shed. A young man, John Roulstone, was visiting the school that day and next day brought in three verses which he had written about the incident. Mary's mother knitted two pairs of socks from the lamb's wool. When Mary was about 80 years old, the women of Boston were raising money for the Old South Meeting House and she contributed the stockings. They were unraveled and short pieces of yarn were sold to interested people. (Descendants of Job Tyler, p. 193)

Printed in the United States
By Bookmasters